DRIVING WANKER

OBSERVATIONS IN YOUR WANKER CHARIOT

KEVIN HORAK

Driving Wanker

Observations In your Wanker Chariot

Published by:
Clearwater Publishing LTD
Netley Hall
Dorrington
Shrewsbury
Shropshire
SY5 7JZ
United Kingdom

Clearwater
Publishing

Kevin Horak 2016
First Edition

ISBN 978-0-9557769-5-3

To Jeremy!

Reclaim The Road!

Best Wishes

18/10/22

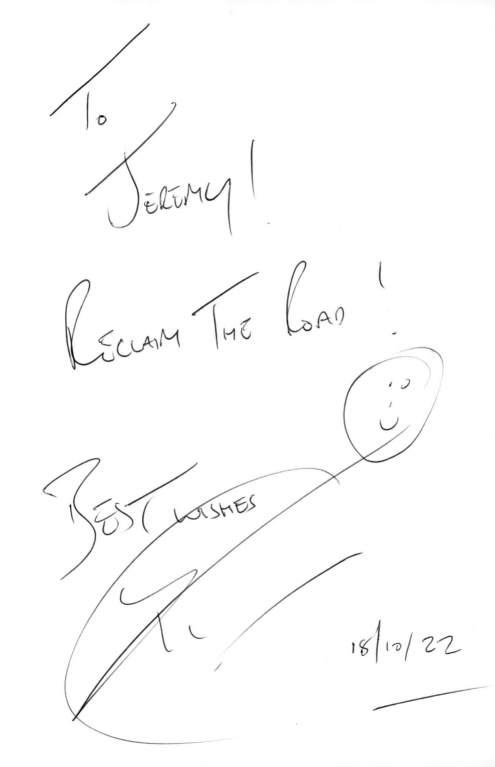

Introduction

So what is it about driving that brings such a colostomy of wankers into your everyday life when all you are doing is gliding along minding your own business?

A worldwide phenomenon that is not restricted to any gender, age or place, if you don't find them, they will always find you, it's inevitable like flies around a turd floater.

Up and down the streets of our fair country there are so many wankers that will interrupt your driving experience it's actually impossible to categorise them all entirely as new ones develop every single day.

In your car, (or your chariot, if you will) it's your pride and joy and your personal space, the very thought of people interfering with this as you are driving around in your non-wanker way will indeed 'drive' you to distraction and your temperance will be tested.

So what can we do about it?

Well, not a lot frankly as there are too many of them, spilling into your path like ants running out of their little colony because the queen ant dropped one.

So as we can't do too much about them or those law enforcement wankers will slap the cuffs on you, we may as well have a laugh at their expense and gain some points on your wanker travels.

So this informative guide is your safety net, keeping you out of court, out of jail and out of the local nuthouse (well it should or you may end up in the second edition).

Throughout the book it is written not just as an observer but also in present tense just in case these things could happen to you, your midlife crisis will start at some point, you never know!

You earn points but alas no prizes, but mark them off along the way entitling you to a wanker spotter rating. If you score over 500 you have earned the right to call yourself an expert level wanker spotter!!

Who could want more?

Keep safe, get out there, enjoy the road and become an expert wanker spotter, there are many of them to keep you entertained!

If you feel that further wankers need addressing please do email the author at wanker@drivingwanker.com I'm very happy to read about your driving wanky encounters.

Enjoy!!

Wanker Scoring System

The beauty here is to collect points as you travel and throughout the book I have given a score for spotting these wankers that upset your day, or even your week; if they upset your life you need to see the doctor for some chill pills and you should get out more (but probably not in the motor).

69 wankers have been identified within this book and a few of them are rare ones, but they are out there as the author has either seen them or has been told about them – so earn your points smile if they give you shit and knowing that you've kept out of trouble.

Some listed here are easy to spot as there are so many driving wankers out there so it's rare that a 10 point score is offered, however, throughout I've offered scenarios that can lead you to obtaining full marks if your enthusiasm offers it.

Earn your points and if you score over 500 you get a gold star of driving wanky spotting – congrats and please do add it to your CV when looking for work – it shows you have observational skills if nothing else.

Scoring

To earn your points as a driving wanker spotter you need to achieve the following:

300 Points or over – Bronze level wanker spotter – good effort

400 points or over – Silver level wanker spotter – very impressive!

500 points or over – you have achieved maximum level wanker spotter status! Long may you enjoy your motoring and keeping out of trouble earning your points, you've won the Gold medal.

Observations Of Wanker Behaviour

Chapter 1 - Inevitable wankers

CHAPTER 2 - YOUNG WANKERS

CHAPTER 3 - MIDLIFE CRISES AND OLD WANKERS

CHAPTER 4 – Rare Wankers

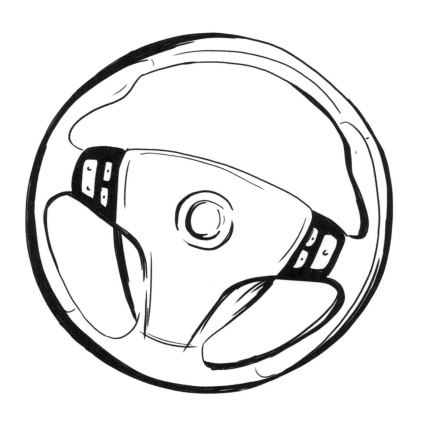

WANK CHAPTER 1
INEVITABLE WANKERS

1. Powered by fairy dust wankers

Eh? What is this sorcery or is it some form of drugs reference?

It may be true that drugs are easier to obtain these days if you watch current media but why these alleged drug peddlers are so brash is a mystery to all with their advertising stickers like they are selling insurance or something?

So what happens if you have this 'fairy dust' exactly because all I can see is a veritable shitmobile with a sticker on it?

At least in the 80's and 90's drug dealers made a statement with their drugmobiles, nowadays it's not so much flash it's just crap – I guess that's modern economics for you.

The dust wankers are a unique bunch of individuals, you first spot them from a distance as their car is usually bright pink.

If you see one parked up there will be the customary row of teddies on the back shelf and inside the car is full of Hello Shitty references and garb.

Also full of shoes and clothes on the floor a moving palatial pimp machine this is not; in fact it's a complete fashion failure.

Keep off the dust and enjoy your driving, drugs ain't cool kids.

Spotting fairy dust wankers: 5 points
Spotting someone from a religious faith trying to help them: 10 points

2. Driving in the fast lane slowly wankers

So if you are of the opinion that the fast lane is for driving fast you would indeed be wrong as that's clearly not what it's there for. It's there for people to drive below the speed limit or completely cock on it, not even 1 mph over.

Who are these people exactly? Of course if you are the vigilant road observant looking out for those little blue lights behind you and those cameras above your head, seeing someone smack on the speed limit in the fast lane you initially have to treat with caution just in case its Five-0 because surely they would be the only ones to do this? Anyone else would be an enormous wanker, in fact a Mondeo of a wanker.

So you approach with caution levelling up with them and you can't see anything that would resemble the filth; looking over you observe some witless fuck of a moron in a world of his own staring down the highway oblivious to everything and everyone. Why this lot of life's rejects have a rear view mirror is anyone's guess as they never use it, they are probably a driving opera wanker having a mental emotional moment.

Also up there for road warrior annoyance are bloody lorry drivers who, in a witless exercise decide to overtake another lorry. If it's uphill by at least a 3 degree climb it will increase the overtake manoeuvre by approximately 17 minutes. Now these dingbats of a Stobbart wankerfuck are getting paid no matter what so why, why, why they do this so they can increase their speed from 60 mph to 62 mph by getting in front of the truck in front of them is anyone's guess – maybe they do it to piss motorists off by causing a mile tailback. If that's their game, they very well succeed. You shouldn't be in the fast lane anyway.

Fast lane hogging wanker 2 points (not much as you always see one)
Lorry wanker overtake manoeuvre 4 points
Lorry wanker taking 10 mins to get past a lorry and failing and
then dropping back (give me strength) 8 points

3. MIDDLE LANE HOGGING WANKER

WELL YOU DON'T GET MANY POINTS FOR THIS AS THERE IS ALWAYS ONE COCK WOMBLE OF AN ASSFACE DRIVING IN THE MIDDLE LANE OF THE MOTORWAY WHEREVER YOU GO – WHY, WHY DO THEY DO THIS?

OK HOGGERS, YOU SHOULD BE IN THE INSIDE LANE, NOW ADMITTEDLY IT DEPENDS ON WHERE YOU ARE IN THE WORLD. I'M BRITISH AND WE DRIVE ON THE LEFT, NOT SURE WHY PRACTICALLY EVERY OTHER COUNTRY IN THE WORLD HAS IT WRONG?

ANYWAY, SO THESE BUGGERS WHO USE THE CENTRE OF THE ROAD, DRIVERS WITH ANGER MANAGEMENT ISSUES GET REALLY PISSED AT THESE TYPES. IT'S LIKE THEY ARE SCARED OF A TYRE BLOW OUT OR SOMETHING SO WE'LL DRIVE IN THE MIDDLE OF THE ROAD SO WE HAVE MORE REACTION TIME, EVEN BETTER, DRIVE BELOW THE SPEED LIMIT.

FOR SOME REASON THEY GET UPSET WHEN YOU DRIVE UP BEHIND THEM AND FLASH THEM WITH YOUR LIGHTS TO GET OUT OF THE WAY – YOU DON'T OWN THE ROAD MATE.

IF THEY OFFER YOU THE DIGIT – JUST SMILE AS A 30 MILE AN HOUR CAR CHASE DOWN THE MOTORWAY JUST GETS BORING AFTER A WHILE SO DON'T BOTHER.

SPOTTING THIS WANKER: 2 POINTS
SPOTTING A ROAD RAGE VEHICLE CHASE AT 30 MPH ON THE MOTORWAY: 9 POINTS

4. MIDDLE DIGIT WANKER

Well we can all do it, so we do (allegedly).

The middle digit is a universal symbol unmistakably showing that you are dissatisfied with something or someone. It's like telling someone to fuck off, they will do just that and off they will fuck.

Like when you give way to someone and they don't even bother to thank you, well fuck you buddy!

Some young driving wankers have other suggestive symbols but when you're a middle aged wanker like me keep it simple or I'm just going to keep starring at you trying to figure out what you are going on about. So if I upset you, flip me the bird, I'll understand that and the point you are making.

The middle digit is not tied to any age group and is understood and welcomed by all. If you've had a lifetime of driving and never received or given the middle digit then you have never driven and clearly a boring wanker. I bet you're looking forward to this month's one time missionary position..........with your blow up doll.

Spotting middle digit wanker: 3 points
Giving the digit because rude person didn't
thank you for letting them go: 5 points
Admitting you've got a blow up doll called Philippa Flaps: (Fairplay) 10 points

5. Make up, check hair wanker

Apparently the use of the rear view mirror is to check what's going on behind you? Nope, it's the portable beauty salon so you can check on progress just in case you're hair has moved as you've driven a few miles.

For those of us who don't have to check our hair I have a tendency to use the rear view mirror for what is going on behind me. But in doing so at every traffic light the driver of the bright red mini behind me has checked make up and hair at every stop, worse still, Fiesta boy to the side of her has done exactly the same?

Not sure what has happened to 'modern man', maybe I need a tribal tattoo to blend in??

If you've ever been a train wanker on your way to work, seeing a lady do her makeup is commonplace, they don't give a crap and the fact that it's taken the whole train journey to complete is no concern of yours – if you don't like it, don't watch, it's the rules of modern voyeurism.

But in the motor on the way to work the grabbing an opportunity at the traffic lights or worse still doing it as they drive; I've seen a plenty on my travels and it's an accident waiting to happen and then your makeup really will look shit.

Get up earlier.

Spotting make up wanker: 4 points
Spotting if she's still in her dressing gown and hair in curlers: 6 points
Spotting modern man wanker preening at every set of traffic lights: 7 points
Seeing the same modern day wanker with a tribal
tattoo – he's max wanker: 10 points

6. Selfie wanker

So you drive a motor? Well done buddy!! But what's the fucking point of the vehicle selfie every time you get in the car exactly???

So what amazing thing has happened in your life now? Oh wait, I know, you've got a different shirt on, glad that's settled then, cos we really needed to know and there was I thinking you've got your mum's knickers on again.

So we are all getting kinda bored with your selfie pics now, so try and spice them up a bit, keep them interesting or you're getting social media dumped, we are so over!

The following are a few examples of which the author/publisher takes absolutely no responsibility for!!! If you are from the inbred village over the hill that people find by accident but never return from and you have webbed fingers, R..E..S..P..O..N..S..I..B..I..L..I..T..Y (say it slowly) means it's not a recommendation (look that one up).

Points gained for spotting these or doing them yourself:

1. Drive around with an unopened box of Crunchy Nut Cornflakes and that box appears on every one of your pictures for the next month, even when you are doing the sex in car selfie, granted a sponsorship may not be coming your way but it'll get you talked about. 7 points

2. Grab a selfie giving devils horns as the Police pull you over and try to get them in the picture (avoid the one of you crying as they nick you). 10 points

3. Go to the safari park and with a random animal leaning through your window grab a picture like your best new mates. 8 points, with an alligator 10 points

4. GRAB A SELFIE OFFERING A BUTT PLUG TO THE TRAFFIC WARDEN AS A BRIBE TO GET OUT OF YOUR PARKING TICKET...YOU HAVE GOT ONE RIGHT? HAVE A VARIETY OF COLOURS TO SUIT; I'M LED TO BELIEVE THAT BLACK ONES ARE BIGGER. 9 POINTS

5. SEE IF PARTYING SHAZZA LEANS THROUGH YOUR WINDOW RESTING HER BOOBS EITHER SIDE OF YOUR EARS, BONUS POINTS IF ONE ACTUALLY FALLS DOWN TO YOUR WAIST, 6 POINTS. BOOBS DOWN TO YOUR WAIST 9 POINTS

6. GRAB A SELFIE WITH YOUR BONG, BOTTLE OF JACK OR YOUR COLLECTION OF JAZZ MAGS AS YOUR DAD SHOWS UP AT YOUR WINDSCREEN. 8 POINTS

7. GRAB A SELFIE WITH A RANDOM POLITICIAN YOU DRIVE PAST AT THE VERY MOMENT YOU TELL THEM WHAT A TWAT GOBBLER THEY ARE. 10 POINTS

8. IF YOU HAPPEN TO DRIVE PAST ANY MEMBER OF ONE DIRECTION, GRAB THE PICTURE AND PLEASE PLEASE DO NOT RUN THEM OVER.........BY ACCIDENT. 10 POINTS (POSSIBLY)

9. SELFIE TIME AS YOU OFFER HORSEY WANKER ONE OF YOUR TURDS IN YOUR HAND ASKING IF THEY WOULD LIKE TO PICK IT UP FOR A CHANGE INSTEAD OF EVERYONE ELSE CLEARING UP THEIR SHIT. 10 POINTS

10. HANDCUFF YOURSELF TO THE STEERING WHEEL AND AS TRAFFIC ENFORCEMENT WANKER SHOWS UP EXPLAIN THAT MR. GREY MADE YOU DO IT AND IT'S PART OF A SEXUAL GAME.........SEE WHERE THE CONVERSATION GOES. 9 POINTS

11. BUY SOME POWERED BY FAIRY DUST STICKERS AND GET OUT YOUR CAR AND ATTACH THEM TO THE LOCAL TOUGH GUY'S CAR............AND LEG IT BEFORE HE KNEECAPS YOU! 10 POINTS

Anyway that's a few examples of not recommended things to do. If you have some great car selfies that actually really are great please send them to my website.

Enjoy your selfies but stop boring the fuck out of us.

Oh wait, I've deleted you.

7. Ladder wankers

Tradesperson ladder wanker you need to keep your distance from especially if the length of their ladders on top of their vehicle is double the length of their motor.

However, they'll always put a tiny little red rag on the end of the ladder (usually in red for danger!) just in case you're dumb enough to drive up behind them straight into their ladders and them going straight through your windscreen – you knob wocker.

MODERN DAY JOUSTING

Ladder wankers: 4 points (if their ladders are double the length of their motor)
Spotting someone driving into their ladders: 10 points
(as long as no-one was hurt)

8. PHONE WANKERS

When you get to a certain age and can afford a motor with Bluetooth this shouldn't be a problem generally speaking but that's for an old fashioned something called a phone call. But this won't stop the selfie queen of course.

Presumably some form of remote selfie driving technology the Japanese are already working on – it's only a matter of time.

When you are driving for more than 10 minutes chances are you've missed something vitally important on your Instagram or a cock womble celebrity you follow may have tweeted something that is vitally important for you to know. Siri is usually pretty shit in telling you the comings and goings of vital things so a phone check would appear to be in order.

Long gone are the days when phones were for conversation (I mean, who does that anymore?) it's what texting was designed for. If you are in a text 'conversation' and you get the bright idea to ring your mate instead you've just broken the rules of modern day communication, don't do it, that's how you lose friends.

If you see someone being a texting wanker as they drive they are a veritable groin ferret. Now the author cannot 'recommend' you tell them what you think of them so you only score points if you see someone doing so.

On a VERY serious note, after watching too many films online of fatal accidents because of people driving whilst being on their phones and the lives that have been destroyed because of this, if you see people on their phone when they drive they should be reported and a stop needs to be put to this. Too many lives have been lost – cut it out!"

PHONE WANKERS: 0 POINTS FOR SPOTTING THESE IDIOTS
WATCHING SOMEONE LET PHONE WANKER KNOW WHAT THEY THINK OF
THEM OR REPORTING THEM: 10 POINTS

9. I'VE GOT CHILDREN ON BOARD STICKER WANKERS

So, so what, I don't care?

Why are you telling us all that you had a sexual encounter – we don't care at all that you've squeezed one or two out. What you want an award or something?

So basically you are suggesting that we drive more carefully around you? Well to be honest I hadn't gone out today with the premise that I was going to crash into someone today anyway so what's the point of this?

Presumably you would prefer it if I crashed into someone else instead, I think that's the point you are trying to make in sparing your children, ideally I should take someone else out instead?

I probably wouldn't crash into anyone in the first place if I wasn't straining my eyes trying to read your fucking sticker.

Well done on getting laid by the way, it just goes to show that there is someone for everyone.

Spotting I've got laid stickers: 2 points
Spotting someone bumping into the back of someone because they were reading the bloody sticker about driving safely: 10 points

10. Speed camera wankers

Another modern day tax collector in order to keep 'roads safe' – whilst they are there on the grounds of safety (which I'm not principally disputing) what grinds my gears is if you get a ticket, in some areas you are offered 'driver awareness training' but did you know in some cases this goes straight to private business who make fortunes from this? Whatever dick dungeon in Government or local Council thinks that's acceptable is a disgraceful little stain grinder. He's probably on a kick back......well, allegedly.

Did hear a story a little while back that a lad distracted the driver of one of these mobile misery machines while his mate nicked the speed camera vehicle's number plate. They put the number plate on their own vehicle and then drove past the camera at speed again and again so the enforcement camera got a dozen speeding tickets. Don't know if this story was true but it's mischievous genius but also certainly a crime so it's not a recommendation!

WANKER ALERT

Speed camera wankers: 0 points as they are a modern day plague:
Spotting one broken down or with a wheel clamp: 9 points
Spotting one speeding and reporting it yourself: 10 points

11. Parking enforcement wankers

The Gestapo's of the road, the creeping death tax collectors of your local council.

Couldn't imagine getting up in the morning and offering this as my chosen career to society, the boy did well eh?

One time the local warlord who failed Policing College and Military training informed me that I had parked in a disabled bay – why? Because it was next to the post box and I was dropping off the mail which takes all of 20 seconds and then I would have resumed my wanker travels. But oh no, this was not allowed but he did allow me to move to the opposite side of the road right on the bend and in doing so I caused a traffic jam as no-one could get by me – makes sense right? He thus informed me that I should read the Highway Code; I'll give this book to him next time I see that Laurence of a labia.

When paying to stay in your overpriced piss smelling car park I've made a habit of collecting the receipts now. When you have about 50 of them leave them all over your dashboard with the one in date somewhere where you know it is. After about 20 minutes they may find it and you've saved other motorists from getting a ticket – simple, you are providing liberty to motorists and you can feel like you've done your good deed for the day.

Of course there are other things that you leave in your car to give the walking custard launcher something to think about, you can either do this yourself or if you spot them points to be gained:

1. Doubled ended dildo on your back seat: 7 points

2. False teeth on the dashboard: 3 points

3. Have an inflatable David Hasselhoff laid out on your back seats – (doesn't really serve a purpose but you'll never know when you may need it): 8 points

4. A huge fake dog turd on your driver's seat: 7 points

5. A Jim Fixed It For Me badge hanging from your rear view mirror: 8 points

6. A Des O Connor greatest hits CD case on the passenger seat (that will really puzzle him and apparently does exist, I checked, doesn't look like it sells well though): 10 points (thanks for supporting him!)

7. Your membership card for the local swinging club on the dashboard (VIP): 7 points

8. Have a lederhosen outfit laid out on the backseat along with a gimp mask: 9 points

9. A talking alarm that has sensors and when he approaches it tells him 'this vehicle will self destruct in 10 seconds': 10 points

10. A coffin laid out across the back seats: 9 points

The author does not recommend leaving your stash out, a dummy 9mm or if you are a part time hit man, occasional body parts, they give these buggers radios now you know.

You never know, you may find one with a sense of humour – good luck.

Parking enforcement wankers: Points are scored as listed above, meeting one who has a sense of humour: 10 points

12. Tractor wankers

Oh struth, why does farmer fecking piles decide to go onto the main road in rush hour - maybe because he can?

But all the same you oversized plankton you cause a mile tail back. The talking sat nav thingy tells you there is slow traffic ahead – yeah because of tractor boy needing to move his potatoes right at the busiest time of the day.

Only fortunate thing with tractor wanker is usually they only have a few miles in them before they run out of puff (should have put this in the midlife crises section) but everyone else will now be delayed by another 20 minutes, phone wanker will have checked the phone at least 2 times to see shocking revelations of who's dared to put on weight this week.

Thing I've noticed unlike caravan and horsey wanker is that no-one gives them the digit – ever!! Whilst appreciating how important farmers are to our being I'm thinking that it's because you cannot be entirely sure what they are carrying behind them and ever since that farmer pelted shit all over that council building there is a dignified respect.

However, drive faster will you or at a more sociable hour, like 3am – cheers.

Tractor wanker: 1 point
Tractor wanker leaving crap all over the road: 3 points
Tractor wanker throwing crap all over the car behind them: 7 points

13. I wish my wife was as dirty as this – Poetry wanker

Now these days media will tell you that the kids are bored, have no future and that the Government must invest more in inner city social development and the suchlike.

However, still a comedy classic from the 60's the 'also available in white' written by hand on the back of a dirty tradesperson van is hardly Banksy but it also shows that not all kids are graffiti artists or lacking a sense of humour or crack whores for that matter.

Not modern day poetry but the kids are alright.

Unless some middle aged twat did it reminding him that things at home have not been dirty for quite some time.

Available in white wankers, keeping the spirit of
66 alive, or was it the summer of 69? 3 points
Seeing middle aged twat doing it: 9 points

14. Taxi wanker

Not to be confused with Fake Taxi on adult entertainment sites as that's never happened in any cab I've ever been in.......regrettably.

In the old days a cabbie would have 'the knowledge' these days many have a sat nav and questionable conversation abilities.

Struggling to make a living because of that Uber thingy they are pulling long shifts and many a time I've gotten into one and it smelling like a travelling fart machine, mobile home.

Cabbies can also make great get around vehicles for hit men, just check what happened in Collateral although hate to be a spoiler but Tom Cruise messed with the wrong cabbie on that day.

I use cabbies all the time as I'm a social life wanker. It's just the occasional ones that could do with a shower before they start work, noxious body odour never gets the best tip, and it will just make me a tight wanker.

But respect to these road warriors running the dregs of society around (including me). We are not always after a chat about the football, the weather and you are compelled to ask the obligatory "You on all night mate" just keep the gas levels down or the windows open that's all. It's a mild complaint and I apologise for leaving pizza all over your seats, it's a better air freshener.

Spotting taxi wanker cleaning pizza from his mobile yard: 6 points
Actually ending up in Fake Taxi on Porn Hub: 10 points

15. Workman wankers

Oh look, that bloody motorway lane is closed again!

You first observe this impending problem by encountering at least 2 miles of bloody traffic cones before you even see anything (the cone magnet is in one of the only thriving businesses these days, except the funeral business; that's still steady). So the guy who owns the motorway cone business with all of his mansions cannot fail to be annoyed that the bloody lanes appear to be closed for no reason – again!

Oh wait, the twat probably has a helicopter.

Being stuck in a motorway traffic jam is almost now an acceptable thing in modern life and us Brits will whinge about it but do nothing of course. All I do is make sure I have a piss bottle in the boot of the chariot because having to jump out in a traffic jam because you need a wizz is pretty well embarrassing up the side of the M6. You'll end up on social media for sure and with all that pressure your piss performance is somewhat on the lacking side – it was cold alright!! And hope you don't get nicked for flashing because you took so long; maybe the Jim Fixed It For Me badge hanging from the rear-view mirror may need a re-think after all.

So you are mildly inconvenienced by 'only' 3 hours but when passing by the workman holiday resort in the middle of the road it's not so much that frig all is going on its like what was the point of this, what are you actually doing? Tops off mandatory if summer, those buggers are getting a free tan from our hard earned taxes. They even have portaloos in the centre of the road now but I didn't notice a wash your hands basin next to it? It's fair to say our roads are shitty.

It's just the same as driving around your town centre that will have mandatory road works of some kind for 51 weeks of the year (they have a week off for Christmas). If you are a posh bugger and live in a town centre you have earned the right to be woken at 6am as they start to dig the road up. This isn't on the basis of the roads aren't busy then or they'd work throughout the night and get the bugger finished. No, for some reason it's a 6am start and drill for a few hours and take a break at 9am when everyone is up.

Those 3 way temporary traffic lights or worse is 4 seem to take bloody ages and when you get to the pinnacle of what has created this much needed traffic light system, you drive past a handful of cones and a digger doing absolutely fuck all, in fact no-one is even there? So basically a cone security system for a digger.

But it's ok as you may spot a 'sorry for the inconvenience we are working hard to rectify the problem' sign, you what mate? There is no-one there accept a fucking digger with cones for bodyguards. Even the portaloo looks abandoned.

A W.W.W. (WORKMEN WANKER WARNING)

Workman wankers (or lack of): 2 points (easy to spot)
Seeing workman wankers working after 9am: 4 points
Witnessing a digger knocking over a portaloo while someone is in it: 10 points
Seeing someone putting a load of cones outside the driveway of
the guy who owns the cone empire: 10 points

16. Take away driving wankers

Those drivers for that well known pizza delivery company have a lot to answer for as these guys are ruthless don't look where they are going wankers. Classic is the moving in reverse technique, basically get in your car, put it into reverse and don't give a shit for whomever or whatever is behind you because these guys need to get that pizza out quick before those anchovies spoil.

They've missed their calling really and if these guys worked in moving human organs around we'd all get up the hospital waiting lists a damn sight quicker. But at least the take away delivery wanker is keeping the 2nd/3rd & 4th hand car market alive and well. Footnote on this if buying from a car auction, other than the obligatory find out if its stolen, been used in a bank hit and the suchlike. Just check there are no trackers underneath the vehicle just in case it was impounded and the stash wasn't found – or some wanna be Yakuza will come hunting you and then its Grand Theft Auto in real life but you don't gain any points for running down hookers trying to make last orders at the Dog and Duck (If your local is called The Slaughtered Head you should have thought this through).

Fresh up is the pushbike delivery wankers; as if we haven't had our fill of biking calamities on the road there is another one to add to the list.

Passed by one the other day going up a hill puffing and panting, the smell of pizza wafting up his hooter probably doesn't help. If I did that job think I'd be tempted to cover said paying client by the time I got there with his moderately warm 12" Dixie Normus for making me bike up that bloody hill, Christ if he didn't give a tip that 2 wheeled cruising wagon would become a wrecking machine!

I won't be applying anytime soon.

Spotting pizza guy wanker reversing into cars: 5 points
Watching biking delivery wanker having a fanny fit because he didn't
get a tip: 10 points

17. Need to move that table wanker

This is not the flat packed IKEA wanker, this wanker comes self assembled.

This road wanker fell all the way through the commonsense tree, banged their head and their brains got rooted in stupidity next to the rotten dog turds.

First observation and motoring failure is that a Fiat Panda is not considered in the trade as a professional removal vehicle but I'm sure others will try and prove me wrong on this one.

Now, I'm not a maths or even a physics expert but your old Nan's 15 feet dining table is really going to struggle in the Panda chariot even if you've invested in the executive version and the back seats go all the way down.

So to attempt this they need a few things to secure this much needed table:

1. Rope, loads of it, often tied around the table and boot lid which is now at a 180 degree angle.

2. If you don't have rope it will probably be fishing line – the invisible stuff that fish apparently can't see so you really scare the crap out of us that it will fall out at any time.

3. Gaffer tape – the tape of DIY kings; anything can be solved with gaffer tape; you'll need at least 8 rolls though as you have the wrap the whole back end of the car.

4. Be observant for smoke coming out the back where they've also fixed the gaffer tape to the exhaust as well...........ho hum.

5. On passing them by you can observe usually a teenager who got conned into picked up the table or the family dog sitting on the other end of it to keep it in the car like some form of counterbalance.

6. As a failsafe they may add a red banner or rag off one of the table legs to warn you that they are driving with a table.........like you couldn't see someone driving with a fucking 15 feet table out the back of their motor.

7. With table legs everywhere observe if they go over a bump in the road and one of the legs goes through the rear windscreen.

8. Extra points gained for seeing the Police pull them over for dangerous driving or for not having an 'abnormal load' sign on the back of their car.

NEXT WEEKEND THEY RETURN TO GET ALL OF THE 12 CHAIRS TO GO WITH IT.......SIGH

TABLE WANKER: 3 POINTS
TABLE WANKER WITH A BROKEN WINDSCREEN: 8 POINTS
TABLE WANKER GETTING NICKED BY THE POLICE: 10 POINTS

18. Parking so close so no-one can get back in to their car wankers

Oh Christ, these, buggers..............

Admittedly parking can be a difficult thing in a busy city centre. But there will always be the bratwurst of a wanker that needs to get that Skoda into the tightest space and in doing so removes you of your liberty to re-enter your vehicle as they have parked 3 millimetres from your door. They park so close to your car that the Avengers couldn't figure it out as to how you get back in.

Standard manoeuvre in this circumstance is to enter the car like Daisy Duke (look it up kids) and go straight through the windows. How anyone can park their motor knowing that the person next to them will never get back in to theirs is not just ignorant they are a driving wankerwaggon.

So after you've done your Daisy Duke (please send pictures) and been completely inconvenienced by these leave a note on their windscreen – did you learn to drive at the wanker school of motoring?

They'll get the point.........probably.

Spotting ignorant parking wankers: 4 points
Spotting a celebration of their driving ability sticker on
their windscreen: 10 points

19. Caravan wankers

Well it's a mystery to me and a lot of the alpha human race but caravaners (or your RV if you will) are among us and spreading worse than Hitler's syphilis.

I'd rather have the comfort of the hotel even if having to put up with old Ferrari wanker than my weekends in a council house on wheels.

Many an hour I've spent stuck up the rear end of these fuckers (I'm more of a giver than a receiver you see); and without having to resort to banging my very impressive horn or flashing my lights asking them to pull over. How it is these road hogging asses of a wankertraveller can just breeze along the road and not notice the 5 mile tail back they leave in their wake?

They say ignorance is bliss, well these shit lords of the dark side of driving are ignorant excelsis.

This is why many of us choose to live in Great Britain, purely because we have no summer to keep these buggers to a minimum — France you are most welcome in accepting our caravan discharge.

Spotting caravan wanker — 0 points (as there are too many)
Recommending to caravan wanker to go take their mobile portaloo to
France for holiday — max points!! 10 points!!!

20. Car is a moving dump wanker

Bizarrely this is more in the realms of the female of the species more than men. Guys are scruffy, yeah sure and we leave pubes all about the place at home, but for some reason amongst the Hello Shitty memorabilia there is a veritable feast of last month's sandwich boxes, high heels everywhere, rear view mirror covered in lipstick (no wonder those selfies aren't looking so good!) and diet coke tins all about the place.

If a smoker the ashtray will be overloaded with lipstick stained butt ends and you hope they are not one of those sorts that opens their car door and drops the whole load on the pavement - ggrrrr.

In fact the vehicle is such a mess you are confident of leaving it anywhere as no-one is nicking this salami garage of a machine.

This is far removed from the powered by fairy dust wankers and despite all the teddies in line on the rear shelf (that must be glued down by their asses) their cars are kinda cared for on the outside

Your chariot is likely to get served with a destruction notice within the month.

Seeing fairy dust wanker trying to rip the glued down teddies off the rear shelf of the car as she's finally met someone (probably her supplier): 8 points
Putting a notice on dump wankers car that they have won a free years sponsorship with Pot Noodle: 9 points
Watching someone lose their shit with dump wanker as they just emptied their ashtray on the pavement: 10 points

21. Jogging wankers

The fitness types are all well and good and not really a driving interference, more of an observational quality really.

Not like those speed walking guys in their short shorts with the backside swinging to and fro – I mean, you want to get into sport, get healthy? – great; I know, I'll walk along roads so fast like I've got a ferret in my shorts and try and shake it about in my pants – what exactly is happening here???

There is no way to look cool in this sporting scenario, doesn't matter who you are.

Anyway; the running folk can earn you points on your wanker travels so look out for these:

1. Jogging in a shell suit (circa 1980) and probably an original as they were outlawed some years back on the grounds of good taste along with your Gary Glitter collection – nope, we don't wanna be in your gang, thank you.

2. Joggers running with those water bottles that fit over their hand like a boxing glove holding only about a third of a pint of water – what's the point of this and it's the worst knuckle duster ever?

3. Headphone jogging wanker – completely oblivious to what is going on around them and the killer clown approaching them – if you can't hear what's going on around you, you are a danger to yourself, let alone anyone else.

4. Vomiting jogger – not to be laughed at (ahem) as everyone starts somewhere; this is more like the hungover jogging wanker, offer them cheesy chips with curry sauce and see where that goes.

5. Jogging club wankers – a veritable procession of fit people all in his and her matching combos or having their very cool nick names printed on the back such as 'long legs Sal' 'go faster frank', 'dogging Dave' etc etc.

6. The jogging distraction wanker – this is the one who is really fit!! So fit that she glides along the path like she was walking on water, her clothing is immaculate, her hair flows freely and whilst you're trying to think of some other beautiful analogy to describe her you crash into the back of the car in front of you..........................you stupid twat!!!!

She then continues to run past your wrecked chariot totally oblivious that your pervy nature caused this in the first place.

Just a thought but on the insurance forms don't put 'was checking out ass' – just saying or 'butt surfing' for that matter.

Spotting shell suit wankers: 5 points
The jogger vomiter wanker: 7 points
Actually seeing someone with a name like 'dogging dave' on his shirt
(don't use this as an excuse to your wife that you were in that abandoned car park because you wanted extra points!) 9 points
Witnessing someone running up the back end of another whist checking out ass: 10 points

22. PUSH BIKE WANKERS

Gggrrrrr the two wheeled mobile machine that can't outrun a Stanna stairlift.

The sporty push bike types have got their shit sorted and rarely a driving inconvenience unless they are in a lycra orgy and there are hundreds of the buggers.

As every man should own his castle not every man should own the road when you are on a two wheeled dandy horse.

These modern day mavericks take to the road with their shinny gear and now come complete with a head camera so they can record the abuse they get because they've caused a mile tail back because they 'wanted to get out there' and burn 100 calories.

Whilst they may appear as completely selfish in their pursuit of wanting to ride along the busiest 'A' road in rush hour, it's the other drivers that seem shit scared of passing by them like they've got some form of catchable venereal disease that holds everything up.

Jogging wanker you can pass by, but oh no, not push bike wanker. For some reason he needs an Olympic swimming pool length to the side of him before you can move forward such is the respect that old person driving wanker will show them.

Often devoid of the Highway Code these buggers own the road and in cities can be seen wearing some form of gas mask apparel when they ride around – they clearly have not experienced my farting fit incident in my chariot, they are actually safer outside in the smog by comparison.

You gain points for spotting loving daddy bear with a kid bike trailer dragging behind him like he's got a portable wendy house on the back of his 'mountain' bike (it's the high street mate, no mountain bike required).

WHAT IS GOING ON HERE EXACTLY? IF YOU WANT TO TAKE THE KID OUT, GET IN THE CAR, GO FOR A WALK OR BE BUS WANKER. WHY DRAG THE KID AROUND WHEN EVERYONE LOOKS AT IT AND GOES "POOR LITTLE BASTARD" LOOKING RIDICULOUS IN THE BRIGHT YELLOW MOVING POTTY AND BET YOUR LIFE GOT A STUPID LOOKING HELMET ON TO MATCH THE TRAILER AS WELL. YOU MAY BE PROUD OF YOUR BREEDING SKILLS MATE BUT THAT KID IS MOVING OUT FROM HOME AS SOON AS HE CAN.

ANYWAY, FOR WHEREAS THERE IS THE LONELY CYCLIST THEY ALSO COME IN SMALL PACKS WITH THE ALPHA UP FRONT. FOR SOME COMPLETELY INEXPLICABLE REASON AT SOME POINT THEY NEED TO HOOK UP IN THEIR 2'S AND 3'S AND HOG THE ROAD IN A FORMATION LIKE THE RED ARROWS NOT GIVING TWO FUCKS AS TO WHO IS BEHIND THEM. IF A DRIVER BANGS THE HORN OR OFFERS THEM THE MIDDLE DIGIT THEY GET VERY UNHAPPY WITH THIS ACCUSING YOU OF BEING A BICYCLE RACIST.

OF COURSE IF THEY WERE AS QUICK TO SIGNAL WHICH DIRECTION THEY ARE GOING INSTEAD OF THEM OFFERING THE MIDDLE FINGER IN YOUR DIRECTION THERE WOULD BE A LOT MORE PEACE AND TOLERANCE. MANY CITIES HAVE CYCLE LANES BUT FOR SOME REASON THEY SEEM TO BE USED BY BUSES AND CABS, MAYBE THE CYCLE GUYS THINK THIS IS THE POOR MAN'S WAY TO RIDE THE ROAD AS ON MANY OCCASIONS THEY DON'T SEEM TO USE IT. I'VE TRIED THESE LANES IN MY CHARIOT AND ALL I'VE GOT IS A FINE.

BORN OF FREEDOM THEIR PART TIME ACTIVITIES CAN ALSO INCLUDE THE USE OF A SEGWAY (BECAUSE THAT'S REALLY COOL, RIGHT?) AND THEY WILL WHIZZ AROUND YOUR HIGH STREET AND IF NOT GETTING IN YOUR WAY IT'S SOME SORT OF CHARITY THING AND THEY ZIP ON UP UPON YOU LIKE KIDS DESPERATE TO SIT ON SANTA'S KNEE AT CHRISTMAS (HE'S ON DAY RELEASE). HOWEVER THIS PROBLEM CAN BE SOLVED BECAUSE TECHNOLOGY IS WITH US!!

ALAS THE MAJOR COMPANIES SUPPRESS THIS FOR FEAR OF DAMAGING THE PUSH BIKE INDUSTRY BUT FOR ME AS A HUMBLE MOTORING GUY WE SHOULD SUPPORT THIS FINE INITIATIVE AND THE HOVERBOARD FROM BACK TO THE FUTURE SHOULD FINALLY BE PUT INTO PRODUCTION.

Personally speaking I'm not fussed about the automatic lace up pumps but there is a much needed place in society for the hoverboard.

I wish Parliament would get behind this needed technology and not stop the development of this master piece of the air as it would free up our push bike problems as we wouldn't need them anymore – there can still be a hoverboard national race sport so pushbike critics can wind their neck in.

I guess the problem is there isn't much room for corporate sponsorship on those boards along with not needing those funny go faster pointy hats – that's capitalism I guess.

Bring forward the hoverboard and our road problems are saved!!

Kid trailer smiling daddy wanker: 4 points
Observing pushbike wanker not using the cycle lane: 5 points
Inventing the hoverboard: Please accept my hand in marriage: 10 points

23. Horsey wankers

Oh to be rich and own a horse and get out in the country, enjoying the fresh air and be at one with nature..........nope I'll take it out down the road and spend 200 grand on some sort of horse tardis driving machine instead.

In the old days horses had a perfect and practical road use and chariot racing of course is what started boy racers off around your town centre every Friday night.....I blame the Greeks.

So we know that they serve no practical road use but for some reason these equestrian wankerhoofs insist on moving them around using our bloody roads!

With the development of drone technology this could be a thing of the past of course and as well as your shopping, woman's weekly and your sex toys flying overhead (still looking forward to seeing the flying dildo zipping past your motor), drones flying horses around much like the purpose of hoverboards for pushbike wanker would serve a practical use.

In fact from classic Hollywood memorabilia of "I'll see you on the battlefield" in the future could be "I'll see you on my horse flying somewhere over the A49" – admittedly the script may need some work. But before you know it the Quidditch World Cup is a possibility and the kids would love it so drone technology us driving wankers should support.

So trotting Nelly is not so much of a hassle but of course like pushbike wanker still needs an Olympic size swimming pool room in order to get by.

However, in modern day culture, if you own a dog and it takes a dump you pick it up, in fact you could get fined if you don't. Now I've got to be honest here as I don't know how they enforce this? If I see someone with a camera hiding in the bushes of my local park law enforcement wankers will be having a chat with him pronto.

So, if harmless Nelly is taking a trot down the road outside your wanker palace and if she has the trots and leaves that dump all over the bloody road, when was the last time you saw horsey wanker get off his stead with a little plastic bag and pick that shit up??

No! It never happens.........

So it's the bloody arrogance of these types of witless fucks who go about their business not caring about the mobile dump machine they are sitting on and it doesn't matter what expensive attire they are wearing they still leave their crap behind them as a modern day shit stain road marker, it's probably for us commoners to pick up anyway.

Next up is they need to put their valuable thoroughbred (lol) in their portable horse taxi, often more palatial than at least the best 3 star hotel you last stayed in. For some reason these machines can't drive any faster than 40mph no matter what road they are on and no matter what the road conditions are, God forbid if there is a bump in the road approaching. This for me as a driving wanker is a conundrum, they ride these things as fast as they can, jumping over fences as high as they can but for some reason with an approaching bend they need to slow up to 15mph?

Everyone has rights to the road, I get that, but horsetaxiwanker needs to Jenson the Button up somewhat and if you ride horsey as fast as you can the driving skills to suit would be appreciated.

Amen, my work here is done.

No points for your journey being delayed by horse
wankers as it's inevitable: 0 points
Max points if you ask horsey wanker to pick his shit up: 10 points

24. God is my passenger wanker

Having faith can be a good thing and the fact that I do the lottery every week shows a certain amount of faith on my part, but those thieving bastards just take my money.

The only passenger I have is my dogs who constantly look bemused about the amount of profanity I use when driving because of horsey and pushbike wanker.

The God stickers very similar to "I've got kids on board" seem more of a warning than anything else? If you see them talking to their imaginary friend as they are driving don't call the Police, call the local shrink for them.

So if you bump into these fuckers does that mean you're condemned to a higher plain or do they take the higher moral ground because they go to church, what's the point of this exactly, it's great that your happy and everything but you know........?

I don't think so Ned Flanders lover; I have the same rights to the road as you and if God is indeed your passenger he'll probably tell you what a twat you've been for driving like Miss Daisy 20mph below the speed limit. I'm not an expert but if you do speed I don't think you have to say an extra 20 Hail Mary's for that?

If you show up to confession and all you've got to say is that "Father, I'm sorry I got close to the speed limit this week", it's no wonder the Priest's end up on the altar wine afterwards rethinking his life and that he could be helping children elsewhere.......I'll just leave that there.

Christ (sorry) get out there and enjoy your life; your wanker chariot is your own and it is possible to do the speed limit and not offend him who is apparently above, he's probably more disappointed with your pornography collection that had you told 'Father' about in confession you'd probably find him more attentive.

52

If you've ever seen the film The Shawshank Redemption the irony is not lost on us that a ROCKhammer was used inside the holy book, "Salvation lies within"; find your own salvation and drive at a more appropriate speed and listen to ROCK, which was clearly the point of the film in the first place.

Start gently with Brian Adams and gradually work your way up to Slayer and Cannibal Corpse via Cradle Of Filth, (avoiding Nickleback of course).

South of Heaven awaits for you and you are now a head banging wanker. Music is the only passenger you need and you can hold your head high when drum and bass wanker pulls up alongside you – you are both in tune in noise appreciation and the slow driving Mondeo wanker of the past is gone and the kids will think you're ok, they are also less likely to dump on your driveway on Halloween......as they have been for the last few years.

When you go back to confession; your priest no doubt will be more enlightened by your misgivings and you enjoy those Hail Mary's..........you've earned them.

GOD DRIVING WANKER: 3 POINTS
GOD DRIVING WANKER PLAYING SLAYER'S 'ANGEL OF DEATH' 10 POINTS

WANK CHAPTER 2
YOUNG WANKERS

25. STONER WANKERS

For some reason there is never enough food available stopping off at the garage if stoned, general munchies include crisps, chocolate bars, out of date sandwiches and washed down with toilet duck.

Stoner wankers can be much worse than slow driving wankers, gripping the wheel if their life depended on it. Often in silence as music can spoil the ambiance (unless it's Acid Jazz or Trip Hop).

So as your driving down the road at 20mph going "Weeeeee, this is so cool" etc the flashing lights coming up behind you is like being at a concert again, Led Zep were good right, cool.

The filth do not take too kindly to your mellow mood with crisps and sherbet dib dab all over you like you'd sneezed a bag full of coke over your crotch so off to the station you will go. As they put you in the back of the panda car or van they will probably go faster than your 20mph so it will probably feel like a rollercoaster by comparison.

When they put you in the cell there are no free Doritos, your still hungry and your high is ruined.

Best smoke it at home and keep everyone on the road safe.

Spotting Stoner Wanker: 4 points
Getting arrested for anything in your life and be given free Doritos: 10 points

26. DRUM AND BASS WANKERS

You hear them coming a mile off, the shop front windows vibrate on their approach and as they get closer to your chariot you get a vibration on your steering wheel, which if you are married is probably a moment of unexpected excitement.

Whatever this is coming up behind you (ahem) it's going to be impressive, you are expectant of seeing a wanker juggernaught of a machine, in fact a Mad Max procession.

But alas a Fiat Panda pulls up with a sound system that cost 10 times the value the car, windows wound all the way down and through the cloud of puff from their bong your expectant vision of a supercar is somewhat dampened.

Not perturbed by this, you could of course blast them back with some Death Metal or failing that Cliff Richard if you are in the mood for some abuse.

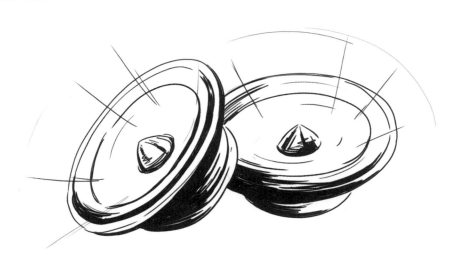

Spotting Drum & Bass Wankers: 4 points
Admitting to owning Cliff Richard's music: 1 point (what did you expect?)

27. LRT WANKERS

If you ever have the luxury of driving around Beverley Hills (make sure it's a supreme wanker chariot) you will see signs saying 'no cruise zone'. Now, not confusing things, this is not like cruising like an alleged George Michael incident, this is when you drive around the town all day because:

1. You spent all your money on your car
2. You have nothing better to do
3. Girls are really impressed with guys who drive around in circles all night
4. You stole your mum's fuel card

However, in many towns the Lap Round Town (LRT) ban has not been implemented because in Beverly Hills if you drive around town all night like a sad wanker you get into trouble – law enforcement wankers watching cameras will catch up with you.

But for most towns who don't embrace the "no-cruise zone" you'll find every Friday night young wanker will drive round and round and round and round – how many times do they want to be seen in their large exhaust Skoda?

But this is a lifestyle, because of economics and the price of insurance now, young people can't afford to go out any more so all they can do is drive around in circles. How they get laid is anyone's business, fact is they probably don't. Chances are Tony from the garage had a pay rise and if he can afford to take a lady out for the evening it will be for one drink only (as well as a few circles of the town).

Spotting LRT Wanker/s: 3 points
Actually seeing one with a date: 7 points
Actually seeing one with a date who appears to be enjoying herself: 10 points

28. Sober taxi wanker

Everyone draws the short straw and someone's gotta drive.

So unless you are taking it in turns or you have a weekly dare competition and the loser drives it's a fact that your driving turn is due anytime soon.

Unless you are a gym obsessed no alcohol beast mode wanker, being sober taxi driver is like going to a long lost aunts wedding that you could do without giving up your Saturday night for, knowing that when you get there a 60 year old DJ called DJ Dave Mix, (the local wedding king pin DJ) will play all of the classics for the last 40 years (well except for the last 20). The Lady In Red just makes you shiver.......

So your drunken fucked up mates who loved the sesh are now in your car with food demands, music demands, wanting you to drive faster, "Can I smoke my shit in here", "Is there another club open" or "let's find the strip club". Good chance one will vom or want to be dropped off at dirty Sal's for a quick leg over on the way back and your taxi session of which they will never offer you any money for took 3 hours to get everyone home.

Get some new mates or claim the car has broken down.

If you spot the sober taxi mate wanker: 5 points
Spotting the same lads getting thrown out the strip club
because they have no money: 9 points

29. Race meet wankers

Well unless you live in a posh place or have wealthy parents it's just never like The Fast And The Furious, in fact it's more like The Broke And Mildly Irritating, in fact your VD gave you more entertainment.

Unless your chariot is totally off the chain what is this all about? The 'race meet' is nothing more than usually a get together of fiat pandas with the occasional Subaru hanging around car parks with piss all to do other than who's got the biggest sound system. The 'race' is usually a quick leg it to the local garage avoiding the old bill.

The flagger to get things going is never dressed like what's on the TV but fortunately 3 fingers Susan had nothing better to do so she'll give it a go just like she does everything else.

Completely pointless yawnathon, save the money on fuel and buy a bigger exhaust system.

Spotting race meet wankers: 5 points
Actually knowing why a lady is referred to as '3 fingers': 10 points!

30. Vaping wankers

It's probably a fad before it gets banned along with everything else that's fun.

These days vapey wankers are cruising around chuffing out so much smoke (well, water vapour) inside their cars that it's a travelling pyromaniac dream machine.

Chances are if you see someone driving towards you and he's hung out of his car window like Ace Ventura, chances are they are in a vape mobile.

Wanker rating for spotting an intensely filled vape mobile: 5 points
Spotting vapey Ace Ventura going down the road: 9 points

31. Piss poor horn wanker

Grown up big people's cars don't seem to have this problem unless they are battling with their own adolescence; this is reserved solely for the younger driver.

When you show up to the crap car dealer with a few hundred in your pocket the one thing always forgotten is to try the horn; so you leave having bought it without realising you've just bought a muffled fart of a horn, terrorising the road you will not be.

Often sounding like one slipped out at the vicar's tea party, it lacks impact, gets ignored, no-one says anything and just gets sniggers.

Congratulations, you've just purchased an unimpressive fart machine.

If someone upsets you brush up on your verbal language skills as your unimpressive horn needs somewhat of a blue tablet to get it going.

If you hear piss porn horn wanker, you've just earned: 6 points

32. Cannabis stickers keep getting nicked by the filth wankers

You clearly have not thought this through by advertising you indulge in the puff with a legalise cannabis sticker on your motor and as wonder why you keep getting pulled over?

Freedom of speech and all that but the 'you're just harassing me' is you own damn fault, having a sticker that 'you follow the Dark Side of The Force' is quite commonplace but if you get pulled over for that it could be misinterpreted that you have a kinky sex life.

Don't be a knob by advertising your drug habit or you'll get nicked, or they'll just take your stash and you'll be forced to buy it back from them at a later stage......allegedly.

Spotting cannabis wanker: 4 points

33. Mum taxi wanker

Your Ford Fiesta has packed up again and the timing could not be worse.

Arriving at your mates yard being dropped off by mum or even worse getting dropped off for a date is a max level wankerability score; she'll think you're a wankerpussy.

Can't afford a cab home? Your mum getting you after said date will result in zero action and a failure to secure a second date.

You loser wanker, in fact a self pleasure hand shuffle is now all your good for.

Spotting mum taxi wanker: 4 points
Spotting mum picking up son after a date: 6 points

34. Bus wankers

The train is ok, the coach is alright if it has a bog, but the bus is a no go area for most civilised people.

No idea what a bus costs these days as I won't be seen on one, presumably still full of bag ladies and the dole gatherers going to pick up their benefits.

If you need to ever get a bus, wear a disguise as being spotted at a bus stop gets you on social media; there is no walking round proud here.

Not many points to be scored here unless you see someone famous at a bus stop.

Wanker rating:
Seeing your mate at a bus stop: 4 points
Seeing a drunk pissing or vomiting at a bus stop: 5 points
Seeing a lad chained naked at a bus stop from last night's stag party: 7 points
Seeing a 'C' list celebrity at a bus stop: 8 points
Seeing a politician at a bus stop:
(very rare as they all get first class travel) 10 points

35. I'M HARD "COME ON THEN" WANKER

NOT TECHNICALLY RESERVED FOR YOUNGER DRIVERS, THIS IS THE ROAD RAGE WANKER WHO SEEMED TO BE INSULTED BECAUSE YOU FORGOT TO INDICATE OR SOMETHING NON LIFE CHANGING.

VIOLATING THE SPACE OF ROAD RAGE WANKER USUALLY ESCALATES AS SO:

1. RECEIVING OF THE MIDDLE DIGIT
2. WAVING ARMS IN THE AIR
3. YELLING "COME ON THEN" WITH A COMBINATION OF CUSS WORDS AIMED AT YOUR DRIVING SKILLS OR LACK OF
4. MAKING BODY MOVEMENTS SUGGESTING THEY ARE GOING TO GET OUT OF THE CAR AT THE NEXT TRAFFIC LIGHTS
5. THEY ADD SUNGLASSES TO LOOK REALLY TOUGH BUT ALSO IT'S TO HIDE THE FEAR IN THEIR OWN EYES – AS THEY ARE NOT A FIGHTER REALLY JUST A DRIVING VERSION OF A KEYBOARD WARRIOR
6. AT THE NEXT SET OF LIGHTS THEY MAKE A GESTURE LIKE THEY ARE GETTING OUT, IF THEY DO AND YOU GET OUT, LET'S HOPE ITS TIMED WHEN YOU'RE JUST ON THE WAY HOME FROM A FRONT DOUBLE GUNS SESSION AT THE GYM AND WATCH THEM SHRIVEL LIKE A PENIS IS TO COLD WATER OR SEEING PICTURES OF DONALD TRUMP NAKED.

YOUR WORK HERE IS DONE.

HOWEVER, IF YOU SEE THEM REACHING FOR THE GLOVE BOX IT'S TIME TO GET THE HELL OUT OF DODGE.

WITNESSING I'M HARD WANKER: 6 POINTS
ACTUALLY HAVING POSSESSION OF NAKED DONALD TRUMP
IMAGES – GET IN TOUCH, I KNOW A GOOD AGENT: 500 POINTS

36. DADDY BOUGHT ME THIS WANKER

So you got born with the silver spoon in your butt, lucky you.

Whereas most of us make do with our first few cars in need of treatment every few months, you've hit good with a brand new spanky right from the start.

So your first car is a Range Rover or with an engine that you're not capable of driving, no wonder your insurance is so expensive as crashing it comes with the territory, not a problem, daddy will get me a new one!

Personal additions when wanker spotting of posh young'uns could include seeing one young lad wearing a cravat along with a trilby to look like max upper class wanker.

If he has a sticker in the back saying 'not Daddies car' – you've earned 7 points!

Their job at the stock exchange awaits – and we wonder why global economics is so bad.........

Spotting daddy wanker: 3 points
Spotting 'Not daddies car' sticker in window 7 points
Having the strength to not yell at them to 'get a real job' or
something........priceless! Well, 10 points

37. Think you've got a pimp/geezer machine

When you've just passed your driving test any machine is a veritable shag wagon – you own the road!

But the insurance is so expensive that the addition of fluffy dice is just not enough such is modern day pressures of looking good.

In the 80's (I remember) thousands of VW's were driving around minus the VW emblem because of the Beastie Boys who were fighting for their right to party (look it up kids), now everything is fixed down so you have to buy your accessories.

Pointers to looking like you've pimped out:

- Fit an exhaust so big that would make Steven Hawkins take flight
- Get tinted windows (although there are laws on this),however, this is expensive so go to the garden centre and buy the backing that goes on the back of fish tanks and tape it to the windows, make sure you get the right one as your windows covered in Finding Dory pictures is just a fuck up.
- Don't whatever you do get some of those eye lash things that you often see on young girl VW Beatles – you'll look like a driving wankosaurous.
- Paint your car matt black – couple of pots from B&Q should sort it.
- It's all about the alloys, however alloys are expensive so silver model paint nails that one.
- Have stick on bullet holes down the side and talk of your experiences driving through 'the hood' and that you know 'Proper' people – you geezer.
- Fit a sound system so loud that you need ear plugs (make sure they are discrete ones) but not so loud that your self stuck window tinting doesn't shake off.
- Have undertray lighting that flashes up and down as you drive around, in the old days that was like driving KITT making you a Hasslehoff wanker (more to follow).
- Always have the windows wound down so you can enter the car through the window instead of traditional doors – girls are really impressed with this!
- Always keep spare sheets, blankets and clothing in the back just in case you have a Pulp Fiction accident – have Mr. Wolf's number on speed dial and check that Monster Joe's truck and tow is open.

So that about covers it, you are now pimped out, now it's just a case of your dress sense and dress to be different. Your car is pumped so get your peacocking in gear as well and ensure your game is good.

Spotting pimped out wanker: 4 points
Spotting pimped out wanker painting his shag
wagon with B&Q wall paint: 6 points
Spotting pimped out wanker trying to conceal a Pulp Fiction incident: 9 points
Seeing Steven Hawking take flight: 10 points

WANK CHAPTER 3

MIDLIFE CRISES AND OLD WANKERS

38. Doddery Old wanker

It will come to us all but driving at 20mph below the speed limit is dangerous within itself. Totally get that independence is important but it's at the risk of every other road user when your marbles start to roll around up there.

If confusing the accelerator with the brakes isn't bad enough, or not indicating telling everyone where you're going, it's the pulling out at junctions without looking that makes my sphincter twitch a little.

Standard old wanker mobile is generally a Rover or an old Mondeo and on first glance looks to be in totally pristine condition as they can afford garages. That's until you look more closely and see all the bumps on the bonnet where they've run down wild animals and the next door neighbour's cat.

If you go out driving and forget where you're going, what each button does or are constantly forgetting your glasses it's probably time to concede for the sake of everyone else and become a bus wanker.

You're probably entitled to a free bus pass anyway.

Spotting old wanker scarring everyone around them, wanker rating: 6 points
Witnessing doddery old wanker driving down the
motorway the wrong way round 7 points
Retrieving the remainders of the cat from their front bumper
and telling them: 10 points

39. Porsche wanker

The absolute epiphany of the mid life crises wanker and confirmation that you are indeed a wanker.... you buy a Porsche.

I recall in single days showing up for a date with a hottie to be met "If you had shown up in a Porsche we wouldn't be going out" such is the feeling of the fairer sex in regards to being seen in Porsches.

Almost like a poor man's Lambo no-one wants to be seen in it despite what it costs.

Have you ever seen a middle aged guy driving a bright yellow Porsche? If you have, he is an off the planet wankatron. You may as well have a sign saying 'married and desperate to get laid' on the rear windshield.

If you actually have the misfortune of knowing someone who owns one of these (and not just the yellow ones), you know that I'm right; buy him this book for Christmas along with some Viagra, he's probably called Simon and works in some form of I.T. as the 'go to guy' for web technology, it's probably on hire purchase.

Porsche wanker: 4 points
IT Porsche wanker (can smell your crap a mile off): 6 points
Yellow Porsche wanker: 10 points

40. Golfing wankers

The golfing wanker chariot comes with its own portable bar as well as other lad accessories – this motor is much more than a portable golf caddy.

Notorious for hanging around car parks in their 4 x 4's with the back end down, the owner sits on this to identify status and their congregation discuss worldly-wise issues. Drinks, cigars and very dodgy socks it's a middle aged hang out for those who don't have the courage to go to a strip club.

Golf buggy wankers are a sight to behold often driving around like they own the place like they are in their very own Popemobile – this is not a place for the great unwashed.

Bragging rights of course because you are in the best member's only club so spending more time 'with the lads' than your lady at home; no wonder when she takes herself out she's now curious by horrible Porsche wanker, you shouldn't have taken so long to get to the 18th hole.......again.

Not many points to be scored here as golfing wankers are an abundant force.

Spotting golfing wanker: 3 points
Spotting golfing wanker whose wife is still loyal to their boring ass: 10 points

41. Lambo wanker

If you've earned your dollars then fair enough; so get an Aston, a Bentley or a cool Audi or something that distinguishes success without looking like a total cockwocker. But if you are looking at a bright yellow Lamborghini and thinking you'd look cool in that you are an utter bellend of a wankstroke – it's not, you'll look a complete tool.

Us driving wankers appreciate the Astons and Bentleys etc but have little regard for a brash display of wealth which looks nothing more than.......a brash display of wealth.

The Lambo wanker loves driving through town centres; not cities so much as it's too expensive in fuel to stop/start all the time – if you run out of fuel and break down in your Lambo prepare yourself for the most abuse you've ever had in your life. In fact leave it, just leave the bloody car and get a bus, just get away from there as soon as possible as your ego won't cope, you have now gone from supercar wanker to bus wanker in one simple move.

So these guys drive through the town at a consistent pace so that people can see them, rev the engine when it doesn't need it and they are completely oblivious that everyone is thinking "that guy must have a really small penis". And that is exactly what they are thinking, so you can look as 'cool' as you like but your new shinny shagmobile is like drink to Viagra; it doesn't work (so I'm told!?) .

The chances of anyone of the opposite sex wanting to be seen next to you is as likely as Donald Trump's hair finally throwing in the towel and getting up and walking off – if you're gay, your fella will want no part of this either.

You have been warned.

Spotting middle aged bloke driving yellow/orange Lambo: 7 points
Spotting middle aged bloke revving the Lambo outside a bar: 8 points
Spotting middle aged bloke in a broken down one: 10 points

42. BALD WANKER

As a fellow baldy I can quote from facts on this subject.

I do the bald, total, not hairy bits around the sides or have a centre spot for a drone to land on, mine is total and total is good.

Why the bald guys have such a mid life problem with this I'll never understand, just look at Jason Statham, Bruce Willis, The Rock, Samuel L Jackson, Kojak and that guy from Right Said Fred.

If you are a fellow driving wanker with your expanding centre spot that's cool but be careful about your new sports car investment.

It's good to enjoy the midlife crisis; I started mine years before due so I could do what I want and blame it on that, it's recommended; also learn to fly a plane, do a bungee jump, try on women's knickers and treat yourself to a wee sitting down, the opportunities are endless!

But alas your roof down in the summer can have serious drawbacks and if unchecked can be fatal to others around you.

As you sweat in the heat and that drippy stuff runs down your head it becomes a reflective mirror that can dazzle other drivers – you are in fact a driving hazard, a blinding light pollutant.

Now this will only last for so long as in a matter of no time your solar panel has not just directed light but also had the ability to absorb so many rays that you'll go as red as your face the morning after having a vindaloo.

If you exit your car looking like a strike match it doesn't matter what you are driving or who you are with, you'll just look like a stupid wanker.

However, this can be avoided with the addition of some head gear, maybe try a cap back to front as this looks really good for the over 40 somethings, trust me no-one is laughing at you.

Knock yourself out.

Spotting Bald mid life in a crisis mobile: 6 points
Actually knowing who the guy from Right Said Fred is: 10 points

43. Posh Jaguar wankers – despise the working class poor wankers

Owning a Jaguar has been a statement of intent for a few generations that you have success under your collar and you don't mind showing it.

Often seen parked in the directors space outside companies or football grounds you can smell the money.

Up until they invented that X class range and allowed poor people to get them so the Jaguar snobbery continues. There was a time when a fellow Jaguar driver would allow another Jaguar driver the rights of the road almost a 'you go first', but not anymore after those louts were allowed into the club. So there are 'proper' Jaguars and a poor person's Jaguar.

If you own an X Class (you poor wanker) and a new XJ pulls up alongside you, you will get a look of utter contempt, it's the rich person's version of the middle digit; if you decide to flip them the bird in response you have just confirmed what they are thinking, you are nothing more than a working class buffoon.

Spotting Jaguar drivers having handbags with each other, Wanker Rating: 7 points

44. Driving with the roof down in winter wankers

So you've got a convertible – good for you!

So you've got a convertible with your roof down in winter – you utter twatasaurous!

I do not drive a convertible as aforementioned due to my gleaming head, but many do of course and with exception to classic motorists with their vintage vehicles it's the masterclass wankers that drive around in winter with their roof down that earn you the points here.

So these guys who drive around when it's a balmy 4 degrees because the motor is cool right? But what are you doing with a big bloody woolly hat on with your scarf fluttering behind you? Ever wondered why people are laughing at you and why your date looks so pissed off?

Add a sheepskin coat and you'll look like Del Boy, if you are not having a mid life moment you are clearly an entrepreneurial wheeler dealer.

Stop trying to show off, no-one's impressed unless you add speeding goggles of course because that's always a winner!

Anyway, fact is you are a wanker; your date is cold and so are you, remember in your midlife that when things get cold it's not just your chariot that may let her down.

Spotting ass idiot driving around with his roof down in winter: 5 points
Watching his date walk off: 7 points
Watching him get the de-icer on his crotch for action: 10 points

45. JIZZING WATER WASHER'S WANKERS

THE TRADESPERSONS FAVOURITE — THE JAZZING WATER WASHERS. IF YOU'VE NEVER EXPERIENCED THIS, YOU ARE NOT MISSING MUCH AND THIS LITTLE GEM CAN OFTEN ESCALATE TO VIOLENCE QUICKLY.

BASICALLY WHITE VAN MAN DRIVER ADJUSTS HIS WASHER JETS SO WHEN YOU WALK PAST HE SQUIRTS HIS HORRIBLE STICKY FLUID ALL OVER YOU.

OFTEN IT'S JUST A LITTLE SQUIRT BECAUSE THAT'S ALL HE'S GOT IN HIM. SO YOU CAN EITHER FEEL SORRY FOR HIS LACK OF PERFORMANCE, OR FEEL SORRY FOR HIM AS THIS IS STILL INSANELY FUNNY FOR HIM.

ALTERNATIVELY TELL HIM TO GO FUCK HIMSELF.

IF YOU SEE SOMEONE GETTING WATER JIZZ ALL OVER THEM: 4 POINTS
IF YOU SEE SOMEONE RETALIATE TO THIS ASSHOLE, YOU GAINED MAX POINTS: 8 POINTS

46. Revving your car to impress the ladies wankers

When you are past 20 years old you think it would be the end of this little beauty of a wanker rating, but alas no.

It's an attempt at alpha male peacocking for the middle aged.

That little tap of the accelerator really gets the ladies going, right? They are really impressed with this display of your prowess - excellent.

As you are probably too old to be a drum and bass wanker, when making your musical entrance being a One Direction wanker isn't going to cut it either so what else have you got left when making an entrance somewhere? You need the revs to get things going.

So get your non-tailored suit on and give your 1.6 litre engine a bit of a go as you park up outside the boozer, no doubt everyone will notice you.

Your chariot has played its part, now the rest is up to you!

Observing the middle aged revving wanker
think he's something wanker: 8 points

47. SUNGLASSES WANKERS

To gain points from spotting the sunglasses wanker, there are 2 styles to keep a look out for:

1. Sunglasses wanker driving around on a dark winter's evening (extra points for a foggy night).

2. Sunglasses wanker driving around town in the summer with his convertible roof down and still wearing shades after dark – this is the pinnacle and you've struck gold as you've just spotted an absolute Jabba The Hutt of a wankerfuck, max points for seeing this go faster shite potato, he probably calls his unused penis Krull the warrior king.

Can't see a bloody thing but damn I look cool

Spotting sunglasses wanker on a winter night: 7 points
Spotting sunglasses wanker on foggy night: 9 points
Spotting sunglasses wanker roof down, summer night: 10 points

48. Dick head number plate wanker

Classic opportunity for a wanker to express himself and tell everyone their thoughts, like what you do for a living, a bit like an accountant having 'tax' within his personalised number plate – accounting knob wanker.

Personalised plates offer that unique insight to a complete stranger's mind so if you ever end up driving into the back of them you know what you're in for.

For example:

DOG1NG69	shows variety in their personal life that could be a conversation opener
1 LOVECOC	tells you what part of town they come from, could be interesting (or not)
RED CAR	tells you they don't have much of an imagination – presumably the car is red
JAY 007	tells you they are a Walter Mitty
SJ AUDI 56	tells you what car they are driving because you are obviously a douche and can't tell
VIL0 ENCE	tells you you're in the shit

The author can attest to staying at a hotel one time and a red Ferrari showed up with the number plate G1RLS – yep, that's right, what a bellend of a thundercock. Not surprisingly a 60 something got out of it, good luck in your pursuit buddy as only Hugh Heffner could have pulled this off. If you see this guy or someone like him, send the waiter over with some complementary Viagra for him and point at the guy behind you saying that he sent it over and make your excuses.

Spotting accountant wanker with TAX written in their number plate: 7 points
Spotting a Sex reference number plate: 8 points
Witnessing free Viagra being sent to the guy who (nearly) has it all: 10 points

49. Doggie driving wankers

Fun stuff to spot when you're on your travels; the man's best friend; other than the guy who invented rechargeable batteries of course.

If you are not a dog lover there must be something wrong with you, you probably have a pet gerbil or something. But it doesn't mean you have to have one but you can appreciate them especially when seeing any of this collection in other people's cars.

Points to gain:

A dog looking like an actual nodding dog: 3 points
Front passenger seat dog looking very serious: 4 points
Dog spread-eagled on the dashboard not giving any fucks: 5 points
Dog going ape shit in the car jumping all over the
seats like its on crack: 6 points
Dog doing a runner at traffic lights and jumps
out the window for freedom: 7 points
Dog leaning out the window at speed so his doggy dribble shoots
out from his mouth on the car behind: 8 points
Dog leaning out of a window wearing a hat: 10 points

50. HIRING A CAR TO GET LAID WANKER

If you've ever done this you are a sad sad disingenuous wanker.

If you've done the big one on a night out claiming that you are one of those rich (w)banker types you've made a rod for your own back. You didn't realise that hiring an Aston for the weekend was so expensive did you?? Well you shouldn't have said you had one in the first place. However, if you ever do hire a car because you were giving the large here's a few tips for you:

1. Remove the 'subtle' hire car sticker off the back, even some plush motors still have this incredibly (schoolboy error).

2. Check the glove box as there is usually something in there to do with the hire company.

3. Make sure you remove the key fob of the hire company.

4. On luxury cars the boot release maybe discrete, find where it is first.

5. When you get to the petrol station (you'll need one if it's an Aston) don't spend ages titting around looking for the fuel cap release button or you'll be exposed quicker than a politician with rent boys.

6. Sprinkle some dirt on the carpet as no car that get used looks like it's just come back from the valet, make it look like you use the thing.

7. Most importantly get used to driving it as performance cars in the wrong hands could be the worst date you've ever been on.

Save yourself the hassle and tell the truth from the start, if she's into you for your motor she's not a keeper.

Only points to be scored here is if you know the person doing this so his wanker score for you is: 5 points
If you've ever hired a car to get laid you are sad, deduct 30 points from your overall total! - 30 points

51. Sunroof stuck when raining wanker

Classic laughs coming right up at someone else's expense!!

If it's vintage, like a car from the 90's or something then they can be excused, but if it's sunglasses roof down guy in winter and the weather is pissing all over his plush interior you gain points at this tool's expense.

Watch his date walk off or run as the case may be. Of course if he's in tune with the ladies he will of course be on hand to provide an umbrella – A Hello Kitty one – bravo.

Sunroof stuck wanker: 6 points
Sunroof stuck wanker and date walks off: 8 points
Sunroof stuck wanker who has A Hello Kitty Umbrella,
if you're gay, go and introduce yourself: 10 points

WANK CHAPTER 4

RARE WANKERS

52. FOOTBALL FLAG WANKERS

FLAG WANKER USUALLY COMES OUT EVERY 2 YEARS TO COINCIDE WITH A NATIONAL SPORTING EVENT.

NOT BOWLS, FORMATION JUGGLING OR A CELEBRATION OF EVOLUTION, IT WILL BE A FOOTBALLING EVENT FOR SURE; A GATHERING OF NATIONAL PRIDE AS WE ALL STAND TOGETHER.

BUT ALAS IT'S SHORT LIVED LIKE A CAREER ON THE X FACTOR AS ALL OF THE UK FOOTBALL TEAMS HAVE BEEN A NATIONAL LET DOWN SINCE DAY DOT. ENGLAND WILL STILL TALK ABOUT 1966 WHICH TO BE FAIR IS QUITE SOME TIME AGO, EVEN BEFORE AN OLD WANKER LIKE ME WAS BORN. REGRETTABLY NO FOOTBALLING SELFIES ARE AVAILABLE FROM THAT ERA.

FLAG WANKER IS NOT QUITE IN THE SAME ABUNDANCE AS THEY WERE SOME YEARS AGO AS FOOTBALLERS GET PAID TOO MUCH MONEY THESE DAYS SO THE MASSES WOULD RATHER SHOUT ABUSE AT THEM RATHER THAN BUY A FLAG, BUT I'M SURE THEY ARE ENJOYING THAT NEW HOUSE THEY GOT RIGHT......DID THAT SOUND BITTER?

SO THERE IS NOTHING TO CELEBRATE HERE AND THE FEW REMAINING FLAG BEARERS QUICKLY DETERIORATE ALONG WITH THE NATION'S HOPES AND DREAMS.......AGAIN.

AS A FOOTNOTE THOUGH ON OCCASIONS OUR RUGBY TEAMS, CRICKET TEAMS, OUR ATHLETICS TEAM AND LADIES HOCKEY TEAM ETC CAN DO QUITE WELL AND A CERTAIN SCOTSMAN CALLED MURRAY HAS WON AND SERVED MORE ACES THAN I'VE SWORN AT ROAD WANKERS IN THE LAST 2 YEARS.........I'LL LEAVE THAT THERE.

SPOTTING FLAG WANKERS: 3 POINTS
SPOTTING FLAG WANKERS SUPPORTING THEIR COUNTRY
OTHER THAN FOOTBALL: 7 POINTS

53. Del boy – car boot fair wanker

The lock stock cigar smoking wheeler dealer.

Granted you don't see too many Trotters Independent Trading Company vans around unless it's in homage to these screen legends but the living Del Boy's are out there.

So London, Paris, New York via the boathouse pub car park, a steal of a deal is there to be done.

Armed with more game than that guy who wrote 'the bible' on the pickup artist industry; before you know it you've bought a cellophane wrapped TV that you haven't plugged in to see if it works and a set of retro flying ducks for your wall.

The car 'booty' often on Sunday mornings at a bizarrely early hour before sparrows fart seems to bring people in their hoards looking for a bargain because those traders don't know what they are doing – right?

If you are doing the walk of shame after your Saturday night shenanigans and still suited (and almost) booted they will spot you a mile off and you'll leave with a shit ton of stuff you have no need for. They may even offer a delivery service for that new TV (good luck with that). Fact is, if you still have some money left from the night before you probably didn't party enough.

If you buy a malfunctioning flying carpet you were probably still in stoner wanker mode but I'm sure you love the sesh.

Spotting Del boy wanker: 4 points
Spotting a stoner buying an alleged flying carpet: 9 points
Chances of your TV showing up: 100 points (it won't happen)

54. Parking hitting the walls wanker

Never got this; genuinely a friend of mine says that she/he (can't discriminate about her) says that he/she uses the walls to know when the car is parked perfectly?

Obviously not a posh twat with parking sensors and probably in need of one of those cars that park themselves.

It's no wonder that destruction of our national heritage is upon us when those historic walls are used as parking buffers, that's if you can get past the dispose your cigarettes here bin of course.

Unfortunately said person also relies on other cars as buffer stops as well. Now that's not to say that she/he is going to damage your wanker chariot but it will be left so close to your car that it's more uncomfortable than your local Priest asking you back for some communion wine for further Sunday 'service'.

Arriving back at your chariot with your weekly shopping you can't open the boot of your car because of this south mouth of a parking legend has crawled so far up your car's rectum that it's not possible while their car is performing foreplay with your exhaust. The resulting situation can often be met with parking wanker having more than damaged bumpers..........just saying, show more respect to your fellow driving wanker, we don't appreciate our motors being used as crash dummies.

Parking wanker: 6 points
Observing parking wanker using other cars as buffers: 8 points
Being invited back for wine with the local Priest; you are clearly too young to be driving, let alone drink: 0 points

55. Flashing Wankers

Now the author has never seen this and can only go by strenuous research for this book on Porn Hub but apparently if you drive long enough in some areas the good local ladies will flash you, the general scenario is you harmlessly drive down the road and some lady in a long coat will show you her wares.

Apparently men do this too – not seen that either......thankfully.

Observing flashing wanker: 8 points

56. Pretty Women Wankers (Me love you long time)

Another ghastly experience to observe when on your wanker travels. They can be spotted working around petrol stations late at night (apparently). They are fairly easy to spot as even the truck drivers aren't interested but it will probably cost you only 10 dollars (Kids, look up Full Metal Jacket).

Chances are you aren't too goddamn too 'beaucoup', in fact you wouldn't touch the sides.

Spotting Me Love you long time ladies: 6 points
Spotting Richard Gere showing up looking for directions: 10 points

57. MULTI-STORY CAR PARKS SMELL LIKE PISS WANKERS

ANOTHER CONUNDRUM OF THE DRIVING WANKER IS NO MATTER THE STYLE OF YOUR CHARIOT; AT TIMES IT CAN'T BE DRIVEN AND WILL NEED PARKING IN A PUBLIC PLACE.

NO MATTER WHERE YOU GO MULTI STORY CAR PARKS SMELL OF PISS, WORSE THAN AN COLOSTOMY BAG FAILURE WHEN YOU CHECKED IN ON NAN.

THIS IS A MYSTERY AS THE AUTHOR CAN NEVER ATTEST TO SEEING SOMEONE PISSING DOWN THE STAIRS IN A MULTI-STOREY CAR PARK BUT YET IT HUMS WORSE THAN THE LAST TIME YOU GOT PARA AND FORGOT TO TAKE DOWN YOUR PANTS BEFORE RELEASE (SCHOOL BOY ERROR).

NOW THESE CAR PARKS CHARGE US DRIVING WANKERS A LOT OF MONEY, I'M NOT SUGGESTING THAT THEY HAVE AIR FRESHENERS AROUND AS FRANKLY A FEW MAGIC TREE LEMON GRASS AIR FRESHENERS IS NOT GOING TO SOLVE IT.

HOWEVER, THERE IS CLEARLY A SERIAL POLLUTANT WHO ROAMS CAR PARKS ALL OVER THE COUNTRY AND RELEASES SOME SORT OF METHANE STREAM FROM HIS JOHNSON, IT COULD BE SAID HE'S A NATIONAL TREASURE AS HE'S NEVER CAUGHT, HOWEVER HIS 'ART' DOES NOT FETCH THE PRICE OF A BANKSY SO MAYBE HE NEEDS TO RETHINK HIS LIFE AND STOP US FROM HAVING TO SMELL THE FACT THAT HE ATE ASPARAGUS FOR HIS DINNER.

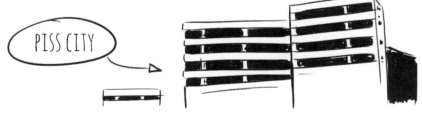

PISS CITY

CAR PARK PISS WANKERS – ZERO POINTS UNTIL HE'S CAUGHT: 0 POINTS
IF YOU CATCH THE PISSING BANKSY YOU'LL PROBABLY GET THE KNIGHTHOOD
OF PARKING ATTENDANTS AND: 10 POINTS

58. Travelling wankers

Not genuinely speaking a motoring nuisance more of a "get off my land nuisance" so observational points to be gained.

If you are one of those wealthy farming types this is your worst nightmare and can be a real problem with the disruption of your cannabis crop – sorry, I'm bad, I meant to say your 'potatoes'.

These buggers take root in no time and can exit just as fast – how they do this, no-one knows. But they claim rights to the land like horsey type does to the road, difference is these buggers may have shotguns and are probably bare knuckle fighters so it's kinda difficult to say "excuse me, per chance would you mind exiting these grounds" – good luck buddy.

They take no shit and the only way you can negotiate is to pay them off or they'll set up camp for the next year, and probably smoke all your puff as well.

The only positive is that they always throw dogs in with deals, and we love dogs especially if they've got hats on.

Spotting travelling wankers: 5 points
Having a bare knuckle fight with 'Mickey' (Brad Pitt) 8 points
Negotiating on behalf of the owner and getting a free dog: 10 points

59. Bikini wankers

Not often observed within these climes that we live in, more of a spot on a foreign driving escape. The bikini wankers may look fantastic but in the heat, skin on leather.........causing damp patches of the wrong sort, in fact it's veritable ass slide in her cockpit.

Also note when exiting the goddessmobile those bright red sticky marks on their legs and of course the damp patch around the ass.

Not looking so good now but good effort.

Spotting shinny ass red legs bikini wanker: 7 points

60. Dental Hygiene Wanker

What the fuck is going on here exactly? You look in your rear view mirror and the person behind you is cleaning their bloody teeth, yep that's right, they don't have a basin at home.

So they obviously have one of those tiny portable size Colgate's you get when you go on holiday, the one that also reminds you that you are single when you book your holiday to Benidorm. Why do people say 'holibobs' by the way, harmless I know, just never got it?

And where exactly does the bloody toothbrush come from – out the bloody glove box?? The same glove box that holds your disused Tom Tom, dust, cat hair and last year's condoms, what sort of good do they think they are doing here? If you ever drive down the road and a load of mouthwash and phlegm comes your way you've got toothy wanker in front of you showering you with last night's curry and the cat hair off the toothbrush.

If you are a bit of a random person yourself and you know someone who does this, ask them why they do it......"Oh, it's to save time in the morning" is the common answer??? Well get up earlier then, no wonder your pearly whites aren't what they used to be.

Bonus points for observing one who is smoking at the same time..........what a catch!!

Horrible toothbrush wanker: 8 points
Observing toothbrush wanker smoking wanker: 10 points

61. Farting wanker

A most unfortunate set of circumstances for me a few years back. Whilst following my mate's car whilst driving alone I had a farting fit that stunk like a whorehouse's back door. My mate signalled for me to pull over as he recognised a girl we both knew walking to work, to my utter disbelief he offered her a lift......in my car. So in she got and froze in shock at the anal pollutant that just went up her hooter. For the next 10 minutes or so hardly a word was said, in fact she went a little green in colour as she was trying not to breath.

Suffice to say she politely thanked me for the lift but never returned my calls.

What a farting wanker.

Moral of the story is you never know what randoms you'll bump into so carry some air fresher or some Old Spice to disguise your bowel problem.

Getting into a farters car: 8 points
Being single and she gets into the fartmobile and
you get a second date: 10 points

62. Stains on seats wanker

This is your grim bragging mate who's been single for a lifetime, a serial player lady whisperer.

His pick up artistry is off the chart or so you would be led to believe as you never actually see him with anyone?

Conversation is always around him and his conquests but his wanker chariot may indeed be just that, a personal wankmobile, no wonder his forearms are like Popeye's.

Be careful where you sit as your mate's sticky residue is no laughing matter when you've got your shorts on.

Having to sit in messy forearm wanker's mobile, you earn: 10 points

63. Giving the wanker gesture and then crash your car wankers

A variety from the "come on then" wanker, this is where you have upset someone for driving too slowly or they just don't like you – period.

Often to be seen as a group of bravado's harassing motorists they travel up and down giving the hand gesture and shout abuse along the way. They never seem to pick on bodybuilders for some reason?

Happened to a friend of mine; he was minding his own business and he received a full plethora of abuse from a couple of young wankers, but they got carried away and as they went past him and not paying attention drove straight into a parked car. To quote Marilyn Manson, now explain those shit stains on your face!

Observing car crash wankers, being wankers
and now don't have a car wankers: 10 points

64. HEAD BANGING WANKERS

WAYNE'S WORLD WANKERS ARE ALIVE AND WELL AND THEY ARE THE ROCK OUT WITH YOUR COCK OUT VERSION OF DRUM AND BASS WANKERS.

MODERN DAY HEADBANGERS DON'T SEEM TO HAVE AS MUCH HAIR AS THEY DID IN THE 80'S WHEN THROWING YOUR HAIR EVERYWHERE WAS COOL, NOW THEY LOOK LIKE RIDICULOUS NODDING DOGS HAVING A FIT WITHIN THEIR MOBILE MOSH PIT.

GUITAR SOLOS AREN'T MANDATORY IN ROCK ANYMORE SO YOU'LL HEAR A CAVALCADE OF NOISE GOING PAST YOU INSTEAD WITH DEVILS HORNS ALOFT AND BOBBING HEADS MANDATORY.

FANS OF JUSTIN BIEBER THEY AIN'T.

SPOTTING HEAD BANGING WANKERS IN UNIFORM HEAD BANGING ACTION (MUST BE AT LEAST 4 OF THEM) GAINS MAX POINTS.

HEADING BANGING WANKERS LISTENING TO BOHEMIAN RHAPSODY: 3 POINTS
HEADING BANGING WANKERS LISTENING TO BOHEMIAN RHAPSODY (4 OF THEM): 7 POINTS
HEADING BANGING WANKERS GOING FOR IT LISTENING TO JUSTIN BEIBER
(CALL THE POLICE AS THEY ARE CLEARLY WASTED AND SHOULDN'T BE DRIVING): 9 POINTS

65. Stretch limo wankers – vomiting Shazza wanker

Ever showed up at that premier looking really cool as you get out of your stretch? Or rather hired one to drive loops in the local town centre – no? Me neither!!

This retro drop of extreme bad taste amazes the motoring community that the 'limo' guys still keep in business. Proper celebrities ditched them years ago and seen now more of a desperate bad night out with only points to be gained as Shazza's ass goes by mooning you out the window (frankly something you could do without if you've just finished your KFC).

The only way of topping this on the grounds of bad taste is gangstaaaar wannabe tough guy's who's invested in the shit of the latest Humvee. But shit he does look with his mobile pimped machine as the only places for the use of the Humvee is in the Iraq desert; something this gangster wouldn't survive 5 minutes in.

In the real world wanna be gangster, the chances are their 'hood' is far more evolved than your local 'massive' and the fact that you may have attempted some sort of Hip Hop thing and wearing a cap back to front with a Raiders shirt ain't gonna cut it in the real world, you need to rethink things, maybe hang out with the God is my passenger guys for a bit.

The times of showing off your wealth with Humvee type's just pisses people off, if that's your aim, you will achieve it, with most people struggling, the brash show of wealth just attracts wrong un's or trouble – presumably you figured that – right? No? Then you're as dumb as you look.

But the stretch limo business will be kept in business as long as there are hen parties with portable vom buckets provided. Vomiting passengers out the window as well as flashing passengers earn points if you spot these!

SPOTTING SHAZZER'S ASS: 1 POINT (IT'S INEVITABLE)
SPOTTING SHAZZER BEING ILL OUT THE WINDOWS: 7 POINTS
SPOTTING SOMEONE IN A HUMVEE THINKING HE LOOKS THE NUTS: 9 POINTS
SPOTTING THE SAME PERSON IN A HUMVEE IN A WAR
ZONE..............NEVER HAPPENS! 100 POINTS

66. Dogging wankers

Well who would have thought that the modern day car had so many uses?

Ladies if you are reading this and hubby has started saying in the evenings that he needs to take Banjo out for a walk and uses the car, be forewarned it may not just be your pedigree Bichon Frise that is getting some exercise.

Gentlemen if you are reading this and the dog is getting more exercise than usual you may need to put a traceable tag on old Banjo and stop spending so much time at your private golf club putting the world to rights or rather being a douche with the boys.

Sometimes spotted in a car park at a nature reserve in the middle of nowhere you may stumble across these while out jogging ahem, (we believe you!) or skateboarding if you are enjoying your midlife (If you show up on a Segway even the doggers won't want to be seen with you).

You can usually tell upon approach and that you've not stumbled upon some form of Druid ritual as apparently this congregation are not all in robes, they have funky looking face masks like out of the film 'Eyes Wide Shut' and 'Legs' by ZZ Top will be played full blast. Billy Joel's 'Uptown Girl' for some reason never gets played – guess this is because it's 'downtown girls' only here?

I'm led to believe unlike attending the Sunday social meeting at the local church, a free chocolate Hob Nob could mean something else entirely.

Spotting dogging wankers: 5 points
Spotting Banjo crying because he wants a walk: 7 points (poor Banjo)
Getting free chocolate hob nobs at your local church (your posh twat): 2 points

67. Knight Rider Wanker – A Hasselhoff homage

Young driving wankers will need to do their research as the 'Hasselhoff' was from the 80's. Back then the car would talk to you; do ridiculous jumps that Vin Diesel can only dream of and had survival skills that would put Bear Grylls to shame.

However KITT was your reliable friend to get you out of trouble and could take on a whole army unlike pimped up Humvie wanker. Not nearly as cool as a James Bond vehicle of course but it was the American showing of vehicle muscular power when big hair and leather jackets looked cool on drivers and not just biker gangs.

But KITT often would try and interject his feelings on the situation and if you are cruising around the dogging parks he may have a view on that (never saw that episode?), it's at the moment that you remember that KITT is an annoying wanker and Michael J Fox's car was way more cool as he didn't' give you any shit and just took you to wherever you wanted to.

But the KITT signature flashing lights on the underskirt is still alive and well at race meetings across the country.

We appreciated KITT but he talked too much and good chance if you showed up at a dogging area he'd probably tell your missus, kinda got the feeling that self righteous bastard would drop you in it.

KITT is RIP not because he didn't have the moves, purely because he was a grass.

Boy racers enjoy your KITT enthusiasm but make sure he's only programmed to talk to you or he'll drop you in the shit.

Spotting a modern day KITT wanker: 7 points
Witnessing KITT and Banjo hanging out to compare trackers: 10 points

68. Lollipop traffic crossing Person (not a wanker)

Now this in many respects is something from a bygone age but you can still spot them with their huge 'STOP' sign to let the kids cross the road in some village and town communities.

Enormous respect to those that do this and give up their time to look after the kids, this is a rare moment of motoring observations that is not critical in any way.

It's so far removed from what we experience on the road with driving assholes and the parking attendants who loiter around your car waiting for that one minute to go overtime. These unsung heroes give their time to protect children and regrettably are a dying practice.

With the exception of the rare one that thinks it's empowerment and will give you a 'ticking off' should you rev your engine too much they should be applauded, although with a changing society they need to be checked that they are safe to work with children. God forbid you want to film your children in a nativity play, it would appear that everyone is under suspicion these days.

Anyway, respect to those who give their time to looking after the youngun's crossing the road.

No wanker points to be earned unless you see one using the STOP sign battering a fiesta because it drove over 10 mph, which will earn you: 10 points

69. Glamorous exit from vehicle wanker

If you spot Shazza exiting the Stretch this does not count as points gained as God knows what will happen as you've seen everything she has to offer already (apologies to anyone called Shazza, the male version is called Kevin if that's any reassurance).

This is the vehicle exiting failures that are rife throughout society irrespective of status, class and the chariot you are dispatching yourself from/falling out from.

POINTS TO BE EARNED HERE UPON OBSERVATION OF:

- YOU WERE 'ACCIDENTLY' AT THE LOCAL DOGGING SITE ON YOUR SKATEBOARD AND WITNESS HUSBAND NOT MAKING A GLAMOROUS EXIT BECAUSE HE TRACKED BANJO AND KICKS OFF...........IF HE JOINS IN THIS IS A NO POINTS GAIN (BUT VERY UNLIKELY). HUBBY KICKING OFF: 8 POINTS
- TAXI PARKS OUTSIDE YOUR LOCAL PUB AND FEMALE OCCUPANT LEAVES THE CAR 'ACCIDENTLY' FLASHES ALL (BRITNEY IS THE BEST AT THIS): 6 POINTS
- TAXI PARKS OUTSIDE YOUR LOCAL BAR AND FEMALE OCCUPANT STEPS OUT STRAIGHT INSIDE A DRAIN AND FALLS OVER OFFERING EVERYONE A VIEW OF 'SATURDAY NIGHT': 7 POINTS
- FEMALE PASSENGER LEAVES THE VEHICLE WITH DRESS STILL CAUGHT IN THE DOOR AND CABBIE DRIVES OFF.............. 9 POINTS
- FEMALE CELEBRITY LEAVES THE VEHICLE AT A FILM PREMIER AND THE CHAUFFEUR DRIVES OFF WITH HER DRESS CAUGHT IN THE DOOR AND REMOVING HER DRESS. CHANCES ARE GETTY IMAGES WILL GET A BETTER VIEW OF THIS THAN YOU: 10 POINTS
- POLICE PULL UP AND STOP THE CAR AND AS THE PASSENGERS GET OUT A GRAM OF COKE FALLS ON THE FLOOR – DOH! 8 POINTS
- POLICE PULL SOMEONE OVER AND THEY ARE PREPARED JUST IN CASE OF THIS EVENTUALITY, THEIR STASH IS TIED TO A HELIUM BALLOON, UPON BEING PULLED OVER THEY LET THE BALLOON TO THE AIR AND THE STASH FLOATS OFF INTO THE DISTANCE. 10 POINTS
- HUMVIEE WANKER GETS PULLED OVER AND HIS PLASTIC 9MM FALLS ON THE FLOOR (DOUCHE BAG) 7 POINTS. BONUS POINTS IF HE CRIES 10 POINTS
- WATCHING A 'CELEBRITY' (AHEM) SHOWING UP IN A LIMO AND NO ONE IS THERE TO GREET HIM EXCEPT THE LOCAL PAPER AT BEST! – VERY EMBARRASSING! 9 POINTS
- WATCHING A 'CELEBRITY' SHOWING UP FOR A PREMIER AND GETTING OUT OF A CAB AS THE FILM STUDIO WOULDN'T GIVE THEM A DRIVER......EQUALLY EMBARRASSING. 7 POINTS

Conclusion

So there we have it road warriors, 69 different types of wankers to earn points from and yet there are so many more out there waiting to be discovered and certainly more could have been included; maybe for another time.

It's important that no harm is meant to anyone if you witness any of these events and getting people off their bloody phones when driving is no laughing matter as too many lives are and have being affected by this every day.

But driving offers us a concoction of some of the most bizarre elements of human behaviour such is the insanity that you see in modern day driving. It's probably no coincidence that 69 is the number that we've landed on!

So collect your points and keep your cool which is sometimes easier said than done.

Keep safe and enjoy your driving, you official wanker spotter!

Oh by the way, if you don't understand the relevance of the number 69 please let me know and I'll write a wankers book about that.

WANKER@DRIVINGWANKER.COM

114

ABOUT THE AUTHOR

Kevin Horak known as Wolfie to his friends is a British author and entrepreneur based in the middle part of England.

He worked as a front line Close Protection operative for over 20 years and ran his own successful bodyguarding business for over 17 years achieving considerable recognition domestically and internationally along the way. He was responsible for some hundreds of private sector security operations including working with Royal families, the corporate sector, the entertainment business and working with grade 'A' celebrities. He made the decision in early 2016 that he wished to retire from the Close/Executive Protection business to concentrate on writing and other business interests. He has written two versions of his Close Protection book 'The New Bodyguard' that has sold worldwide.

In 2006 he set up his hugely successful independent record label 'A Wolf At Your Door', a rock and punk imprint that focused on home grown artists. The label was behind launching the careers of successful artists such as Mallory Knox, Deaf Havana and Lower Than Atlantis to name a few. In the middle part of 2016 he made the decision along with retiring from the Close Protection business to bring the label to a close and he sold it to a much larger independent label.

Nowadays and free of the restraint from working in the private security sector he writes humorous accounts of everyday life. He works very closely with his Fiancé professional model Chilli Chapel helping manage her career (chillichapel.com). Also with living with Chilli he shares his house with two very camp looking un-alpha male dogs and not taking himself or life too seriously any more.

He still enjoys driving...............mostly!

FURTHER WANKER READING

f : GYMWANKKER

🐦 : GYMWANKERBOOK

📷 : GYM_WANKER

GYMWANKER.COM
KEVINHORAK.COM

117